Symbolism of the Corner Stone, the North East Corner and the Religious & Masonic Symbolism of Stones

By Albert G. Mackey, William Harvey and William Wynn Westcott

Copyright © 2019 Lamp of Trismegistus. All rights reserved. No part of this publication may be reproduced or transmitted in any form or by any means, electronic or mechanical, including photocopying, recording, or by any information storage and retrieval system, without permission in writing from Hecate Arcanum. Reviewers may quote brief passages.

ISBN: 978-1-63118-412-3

Foundations of Freemasonry Series

Other Books in this Series and Related Titles

The Story and Legend of Hiram Abiff by William Harvey, Manly P. Hall and Albert G. Mackey
(978-1-63118-411-6)

Symbolism and Discourses on the Entered Apprentice, Fellowcraft and Master Mason Blue Lodge Degrees by H. L. Haywood, Asahel W. Gage, William Harvey, Albert G. Mackey and Arthur Edward Waite
(978-1-63118-413-0)

Ancient Mysteries and Secret Societies by Manly P. Hall
(978-1-63118-410-9)

The Influence of Pythagoras on Freemasonry, the Golden Verses of Pythagoras and the Life and Philosophy of Pythagoras by Albert G. Mackey and Manly P. Hall (978-1-63118-320-1)

The Philosophy of Masonry in Five Parts by Roscoe Pound
(978-1-63118-004-0)

Rosicrucian and Masonic Origins by Manly P. Hall
(978-1-63118-000-2)

Four Lesser Known Masonic Essays by Frank C. Higgins
(978-1-63118-003-3)

The Hiramic Legend and the Ashmolean Theory by W. B. Hextall
(978-1-63118-002-6)

A Collection of Writings Related to Occult, Esoteric, Rosicrucian and Hermetic Literature, Including Freemasonry, the Kabbalah, the Tarot, Alchemy and Theosophy various authors *Volumes 1-4*
(978-1-63118-713-1) (978-1-63118-714-8)
(978-1-63118-715-5) (978-1-63118-716-2)

Audio Versions are also Available on Audible and iTunes

Table of Contents

Introduction...7

Symbolism of the Corner Stone by Albert G. Mackey...9

The North-East Corner by William Harvey...25

Religious & Masonic Symbolism of Stones by William Wynn Westcott...39

Introduction

From the beginning of Modern Freemasonry's birthdate of 1717, the intelligentsia of humanity have found refuge for safe reflection within the walls of the fraternity. Masonic writers have produced a nearly incalculable amount of written musings on a multitude of esoteric and philosophical subjects, as they relate to the ancient mysteries that Freemasonry currently storehouses. Sadly, most of it appears to have sat largely unread, as American Freemasonry in particular, continues to transform itself into something that bares little resemblance to what it was originally designed to be. The true essence of Freemasonry is not that of blind patriotism or a single-minded national religion but one of Universal Brotherhood and altruism, designed for the betterment not just of its members but of society as a whole. In particular, for those who are not members of the fraternity, as Freemasonry has always acted as a beacon, to help guide humanity through darker times, with the hopes that one day we will collectively reach a truly enlightened age.

It's not uncommon for new members joining the fraternity to find little education within the walls of many modern lodges, in spite of so much written material available to the membership. Many older members are not simply uneducated with regards to real Masonic history and symbology, not to mention the vast arena of related subjects, but they are disinterested in all of it, as well.

Lamp of Trismegistus offers its readers highlights of Masonic study, culled from a variety of authors and viewpoints, with the hope bringing education back into the fraternity. So, be sure to check out other titles in our *Foundations of Freemasonry Series* as well as our *Esoteric Classics*, *Christian Apocrypha Series* and our *Theosophical Classics*, and don't be afraid to let a little altruism into your own heart or even into your Lodge.

Symbolism of the Corner-Stone

By Albert G. Mackey

Allow us to consider the symbolism connected with an important ceremony in the ritual of the first degree of Masonry, which refers to the north-east corner of the lodge. In this ceremony the candidate becomes the representative of a spiritual corner-stone. And hence, to thoroughly comprehend the true meaning of the emblematic ceremony, it is essential that we should investigate the symbolism of the *corner-stone*.

The corner-stone, as the foundation on which the entire building is supposed to rest, is, of course, the most important stone in the whole edifice. It is, at least, so considered by operative masons. It is laid with impressive ceremonies; the assistance of speculative masons is often, and always ought to be, invited, to give dignity to the occasion; and the event is viewed by the workmen as an important era in the construction of the edifice.

In the rich imagery of Orientalism, the corner-stone is frequently referred to as the appropriate symbol of a chief or prince who is the defense and bulwark of his people, and more particularly in Scripture, as denoting that promised Messiah who was to be the sure prop and support of all who should put their trust in his divine mission.

To the various properties that are necessary to constitute

a true corner-stone,—its firmness and durability, its perfect form, and its peculiar position as the connecting link between the walls,—we must attribute the important character that it has assumed in the language of symbolism. Freemasonry, which alone, of all existing institutions, has preserved this ancient and universal language, could not, as it may well be supposed, have neglected to adopt the corner-stone among its most cherished and impressive symbols; and hence it has referred to it many of its most significant lessons of morality and truth.

I have already alluded to that peculiar mode of masonic symbolism by which the speculative mason is supposed to be engaged in the construction of a spiritual temple, in imitation of, or, rather, in reference to, that material one which was erected by his operative predecessors at Jerusalem. Let us again, for a few moments, direct our attention to this important fact, and revert to the connection which originally existed between the operative and speculative divisions of Freemasonry. This is an essential introduction to any inquiry into the symbolism of the corner-stone.

The difference between operative and speculative Masonry is simply this—that while the former was engaged in the construction of a material temple, formed, it is true, of the most magnificent materials which the quarries of Palestine, the mountains of Lebanon, and the golden shores of Ophir could contribute, the latter occupies itself in the erection of a spiritual house,—a house not made with hands,—in which, for stones and cedar, and gold and precious stones, are substituted the virtues of the heart, the pure emotions of the soul, the warm affections gushing forth from the hidden fountains of the spirit, so that the very presence of Jehovah, our Father and our God, shall be enshrined within us as his Shekinah was in the holy of holies of the material temple at Jerusalem.

The Speculative Mason, then, if he rightly comprehends the scope and design of his profession, is occupied, from his very first admission into the order until the close of his labors and his life,—and the true mason's labor ends only with his life,—in the construction, the adornment, and the completion of this spiritual temple of his body. He lays its foundation in a firm belief and an unshaken confidence in the wisdom, power, and goodness of God. This is his first step. Unless his trust is in God, and in him only, he can advance no further than the threshold of initiation. And then he prepares his materials with the gauge and gavel of Truth, raises the walls by the plumb-line of Rectitude, squares his work with the square of Virtue, connects the whole with the cement of Brotherly Love, and thus skillfully erects the living edifice of thoughts, and words, and deeds, in accordance with the designs laid down by the Master Architect of the universe in the great Book of Revelation.

The aspirant for masonic light—the Neophyte—on his first entrance within our sacred porch, prepares himself for this consecrated labor of erecting within his own bosom a fit dwelling-place for the Divine Spirit, and thus commences the noble work by becoming himself the corner-stone on which this spiritual edifice is to be erected.

Here, then, is the beginning of the symbolism of the corner-stone; and it is singularly curious to observe how every portion of the archetype has been made to perform its appropriate duty in thoroughly carrying out the emblematic allusions.

As, for example, this symbolic reference of the corner-stone of a material edifice to a mason, when, at his first initiation, he commences the intellectual task of erecting a spiritual temple in his heart, is beautifully sustained in the allusions to all the various parts and qualities which are to be found in a "well-formed, true and trusty" corner-stone. Its form and substance are both seized by the comprehensive grasp of the symbolic science.

Let us trace this symbolism in its minute details. And, first, as to the form of the corner-stone.

The corner-stone of an edifice must be perfectly square on its surfaces, lest, by a violation of this true geometric figure, the walls to be erected upon it should deviate from the required line of perpendicularity which can alone give strength and proportion to the building.

Perfectly square on its surfaces, it is, in its form and solid contents, a cube. Now, the square and the cube are both important and significant symbols.

The square is an emblem of morality, or the strict performance of every duty. Among the Greeks, who were a highly poetical and imaginative people, the square was deemed a figure of perfection, and "the square or cubical man," was a term used to designate a man of unsullied integrity. Hence one of their most eminent metaphysicians has said that "he who valiantly sustains the shocks of adverse fortune, demeaning himself uprightly, is truly good and of a square posture, without reproof; and he who would assume such a square posture should often subject himself to the perfectly square test of justice and integrity."

The cube, in the language of symbolism, denotes truth. Among the pagan mythologists, Mercury, or Hermes, was always represented by a cubical stone, because he was the type of truth, and the same form was adopted by the Israelites in the construction of the tabernacle, which was to be the dwelling-place of divine truth.

And, then, as to its material: This, too, is an essential element of all symbolism. Constructed of a material finer and more polished than that which constitutes the remainder of the edifice, often carved with appropriate devices and fitted for its distinguished purpose by the utmost skill of the sculptor's art, it becomes the symbol of that beauty of holiness with which the Hebrew Psalmist has said that we are to worship Jehovah.

The ceremony, then, of the north-east corner of the lodge, since it derives all its typical value from this symbolism of the corner-stone, was undoubtedly intended to portray, in this consecrated language, the necessity of integrity and stability of conduct, of truthfulness and uprightness of character, and of purity and holiness of life, which, just at that time and in that place, the candidate is most impressively charged to maintain.

But there is also a symbolism about the position of the corner-stone, which is well worthy of attention. It is familiar to everyone,—even to those who are without the pale of initiation,—that the custom of laying the corner-stones of public buildings has always been performed by the masonic order with peculiar and impressive ceremonies, and that this stone is invariably deposited in the north-east corner of the foundation of the intended structure. Now, the question naturally suggests itself: Whence does this ancient and invariable usage derive its origin? Why may not the stone be deposited in any other corner or portion of the edifice, as convenience or necessity may dictate? The custom of placing the foundation-stone in the north-east corner must have been originally adopted for some good and sufficient reason; for we have a right to suppose that it was not an arbitrary selection. Was it in reference to the ceremony which takes place in the lodge? Or is that in reference to the position of the material stone? No matter which has the precedence in point of time, the principle is the same. The position of the stone in the north-east corner of the building is altogether symbolic, and the symbolism exclusively alludes to certain doctrines which are taught in the speculative science of Masonry.

The interpretation, I conceive, is briefly this: Every Speculative Mason is familiar with the fact that the east, as the source of material light, is a symbol of his own order, which professes to contain within its bosom the pure light of truth. As, in the physical world, the morning of each day is ushered into existence by the reddening dawn of the eastern sky, whence the rising sun dispenses his illuminating and prolific rays to every portion of the visible horizon, warming the whole earth with his embrace of light, and giving new-born life and energy to flower and tree, and beast and man, who, at the magic touch, awake from the sleep of darkness, so in the moral world, when intellectual night was, in the earliest days, brooding over the world, it was from the ancient priesthood living in the east that those lessons of God, of nature, and of humanity first emanated, which, travelling westward, revealed to man his future destiny, and his dependence on a superior power. Thus every new and true doctrine, coming from these "wise men of the east," was, as it were, a new day arising, and dissipating the clouds of intellectual darkness and error. It was a universal opinion among the ancients that the first learning came from the east; and the often-quoted line of Bishop Berkeley, that "Westward the course of empire takes its way"—is but the modern utterance of an ancient thought, for it was always believed that the empire of truth and knowledge was advancing from the east to the west.

Again: the north, as the point in the horizon which is most remote from the vivifying rays of the sun when at his meridian height, has, with equal metaphorical propriety, been called the place of darkness, and is, therefore, symbolic of the profane world, which has not yet been penetrated and illumined by the intellectual rays of masonic light. All history concurs in recording the fact that, in the early ages of the world, its northern portion was enveloped in the most profound moral and mental darkness. It was from the remotest regions of

Northern Europe that those barbarian hordes "came down like the wolf on the fold," and devastated the fair plains of the south, bringing with them a dark curtain of ignorance, beneath whose heavy folds the nations of the world lay for centuries overwhelmed. The extreme north has ever been, physically and intellectually, cold, and dark, and dreary. Hence, in Masonry, the north has ever been esteemed the place of darkness; and, in obedience to this principle, no symbolic light is allowed to illumine the northern part of the lodge.

The east, then, is, in Masonry, the symbol of the order, and the north the symbol of the profane world.

Now, the spiritual corner-stone is deposited in the north-east corner of the lodge, because it is symbolic of the position of the neophyte, or candidate, who represents it in his relation to the order and to the world. From the profane world he has just emerged. Some of its imperfections are still upon him; some of its darkness is still about him; he as yet belongs in part to the north. But he is striving for light and truth; the pathway upon which he has entered is directed towards the east. His allegiance, if I may use the word, is divided. He is not altogether a profane, nor altogether a mason. If he were wholly in the world, the north would be the place to find him—the north, which is the reign of darkness. If he were wholly in the order,—a Master Mason,—the east would have received him— the east, which is the place of light. But he is neither; he is an Apprentice, with some of the ignorance of the world cleaving to him, and some of the light of the order beaming upon him. And hence this divided allegiance—this double character—this mingling of the departing darkness of the north with the approaching brightness of the east—is well expressed, in our symbolism, by the appropriate position of the spiritual corner-stone in the north-east corner of the lodge. One surface of the stone faces the north, and the other surface faces the east. It is neither wholly in the one part nor wholly in the other, and in so far it is a symbol of initiation not fully developed—that which is incomplete and imperfect, and is, therefore, fitly represented by the recipient of the first degree, at the very moment of his initiation.

But the strength and durability of the corner-stone are also eminently suggestive of symbolic ideas. To fulfill its design as the foundation and support of the massive building whose erection it precedes, it should be constructed of a material which may outlast all other parts of the edifice, so that when that "eternal ocean whose waves are years" shall have engulfed all who were present at the construction of the building in the vast vortex of its ever-flowing current; and when generation after generation shall have passed away, and the crumbling stones of the ruined edifice shall begin to attest the power of time and the evanescent nature of all human undertakings, the corner-stone will still remain to tell, by its inscriptions, and its form, and its beauty, to every passer-by, that there once existed in that, perhaps then desolate, spot, a building consecrated to some noble or some sacred purpose by the zeal and liberality of men who now no longer live.

So, too, do this permanence and durability of the corner-stone, in contrast with the decay and ruin of the building in whose foundations it was placed, remind the mason that when this earthly house of his tabernacle shall have passed away, he has within him a sure foundation of eternal life—a cornerstone of immortality—an emanation from that Divine Spirit which pervades all nature, and which, therefore, must survive the tomb, and rise, triumphant and eternal, above the decaying dust of death and the grave.

It is in this way that the student of masonic symbolism is reminded by the corner-stone—by its form, its position, and its permanence—of significant doctrines of duty, and virtue, and religious truth, which it is the great object of Masonry to teach.

But I have said that the material corner-stone is deposited in its appropriate place with solemn rites and ceremonies, for which the order has established a peculiar ritual. These, too, have a beautiful and significant symbolism, the investigation of which will next attract our attention.

And here it may be observed, in passing, that the accompaniment of such an act of consecration to a particular purpose, with solemn rites and ceremonies, claims our respect, from the prestige that it has of all antiquity. A learned writer on symbolism makes, on this subject, the following judicious remarks, which may be quoted as a sufficient defense of our masonic ceremonies:—

"It has been an opinion, entertained in all past ages, that by the performance of certain acts, things, places, and persons acquire a character which they would not have had without such performances. The reason is plain: certain acts signify firmness of purpose, which, by consigning the object to the intended use, gives it, in the public opinion, an accordant character. This is most especially true of things, places, and persons connected with religion and religious worship. After the performance of certain acts or rites, they are held to be altogether different from what they were before; they acquire a sacred character, and in some instances a character absolutely divine. Such are the effects imagined to be produced by religious dedication."

The stone, therefore, thus properly constructed, is, when it is to be deposited by the constituted authorities of our order, carefully examined with the necessary implements of operative masonry,—the square, the level, and the plumb,—and declared to be "well-formed, true, and trusty." This is not a vain nor unmeaning ceremony. It teaches the mason that his virtues are to be tested by temptation and trial, by suffering and adversity, before they can be pronounced by the Master Builder of souls to be materials worthy of the spiritual building of eternal life, fitted "as living stones, for that house not made with hands, eternal in the heavens." But if he be faithful, and withstand these trials,—if he shall come forth from these temptations and sufferings like pure gold from the refiner's fire,—then, indeed, shall he be deemed "well-formed, true, and trusty," and worthy to offer "unto the Lord an offering in righteousness."

In the ceremony of depositing the corner-stone, the sacred elements of masonic consecration are then produced, and the stone is solemnly set apart by pouring corn, wine, and oil upon its surface. Each of these elements has a beautiful significance in our symbolism.

Collectively, they allude to the Corn of Nourishment, the Wine of Refreshment, and the Oil of Joy, which are the promised rewards of a faithful and diligent performance of duty, and often specifically refer to the anticipated success of the undertaking whose incipiency they have consecrated. They are, in fact, types and symbols of all those abundant gifts of Divine Providence for which we are daily called upon to make an offering of our thanks, and which are enumerated by King David, in his catalogue of blessings, as "wine that maketh glad the heart of man, and oil to make his face to shine, and bread which strengtheneth man's heart."

"Wherefore, my brethren," says Harris, "do you carry *corn, wine, and oil* in your processions, but to remind you that in the pilgrimage of human life you are to impart a portion of your bread to feed the hungry, to send a cup of your wine to cheer the sorrowful, and to pour the healing oil of your consolation into the wounds which sickness hath made in the bodies, or affliction rent in the hearts, of your fellow-travellers?"

But, individually, each of these elements of consecration has also an appropriate significance, which is well worth investigation.

Corn, in the language of Scripture, is an emblem of the resurrection, and St. Paul, in that eloquent discourse which is so familiar to all, as a beautiful argument for the great Christian doctrine of a future life, adduces the seed of grain, which, being sown, first dieth, and then quickeneth, as the appropriate type of that corruptible which must put on incorruption, and of that mortal which must assume immortality. But, in Masonry, the sprig of acacia, for reasons purely masonic, has been always adopted as the symbol of immortality, and the ear of corn is appropriated as the symbol of plenty. This is in accordance with the Hebrew derivation of the word, as well as with the usage of all ancient nations. The word *dagan*, דגן which signifies *corn*, is derived from the verb *dagah*, דגה, *to increase, to multiply*, and in all the ancient religions the horn or vase, filled with fruits and with grain, was the recognized symbol of plenty. Hence, as an element of consecration, corn is intended to remind us of those temporal blessings of life and health, and comfortable support, which we derive from the Giver of all good, and to merit which we should strive, with "clean hands and a pure heart," to erect on the corner-stone of our initiation a spiritual temple, which shall be adorned with the "beauty of holiness."

Wine is a symbol of that inward and abiding comfort with which the heart of the man who faithfully performs his part on the great stage of life is to be refreshed; and as, in the figurative language of the East, Jacob prophetically promises to Judah, as his reward, that he shall wash his garments in wine, and his clothes in the blood of the grape, it seems intended, morally, to remind us of those immortal refreshments which, when the labors of this earthly lodge are forever closed, we shall receive in the celestial lodge above, where the G.A.O.T.U. forever presides.

Oil is a symbol of prosperity, and happiness, and joy.

The custom of anointing every thing or person destined for a sacred purpose is of venerable antiquity. The statues of the heathen deities, as well as the altars on which the sacrifices were offered to them, and the priests who presided over the sacred rites, were always anointed with perfumed ointment, as a consecration of them to the objects of religious worship.

When Jacob set up the stone on which he had slept in his journey to Paddan-aram, and where he was blessed with the vision of ascending and descending angels, he anointed it with oil, and thus consecrated it as an altar to God. Such an inunction was, in ancient times, as it still continues to be in many modern countries and contemporary religions, a symbol of the setting apart of the thing or person so anointed and consecrated to a holy purpose.

Hence, then, we are reminded by this last impressive ceremony, that the cultivation of virtue, the practice of duty, the resistance of temptation, the submission to suffering, the devotion to truth, the maintenance of integrity, and all those other graces by which we strive to fit our bodies, as living stones, for the spiritual building of eternal life, must, after all, to make the object effectual and the labor successful, be consecrated by a holy obedience to God's will and a firm reliance on God's providence, which alone constitute the chief corner-stone and sure foundation, on which any man can build with the reasonable hope of a prosperous issue to his work.

It may be noticed, in concluding this topic, that the corner-stone seems to be peculiarly a Jewish symbol. I can find no reference to it in any of the ancient pagan rites, and the EBEN PINAH, the *corner-stone*, which is so frequently mentioned in Scripture as the emblem of an important personage, and most usually, in the Old Testament, of the expected Messiah, appears, in its use in Masonry, to have had, unlike almost every other symbol of the order, an exclusively temple origin.

The North East Corner

PREFACE

As a Humble student of the mysteries of our ancient fraternity I have often felt that the solemnity and significance of the N.E. Corner Charge are marred to some extent by the undue emphasis which is put upon one meaning of the word "Charity" to the practical exclusion of all others. I find that other brethren have been similarly impressed. As a Result of discussions on the matter I have prepared the following Lecture which I hope will be accepted as an attempt, at least, towards an exposition of the subject in its varies aspects.

WILLIAM HARVEY
4 Gowrie Street
Dundee

The North-East Corner

By William Harvey

I have heard it said by men who have travelled far in Freemasonry that no degree excels the First; and that of the First, the N.E. Corner charge is unequalled by any other portion of our finely-phrased ceremonial. The First Degree has all the charm of novelty and surprise. As a rule, the uninitiated knows nothing of our ritual, and is in a state of total darkness as to our order of service. He may have picked up little bits of information from a variety of more or less authentic sources, but these, most probably, have been intermixed with suggestions that the whole ceremony is a species of horseplay in which more or less good-natured buffoonery has a conspicuous part. As a consequence, the candidate approaches the business in a kind of spirit of derring-do, fortified by the reflection that, as many of his friends and acquaintances have survived the ordeal, he may have similar luck. To a mind thus prepared, or, unprepared, our ceremonial must come as a sort of spiritual revelation. The candidate finds himself at once in an atmosphere vastly different from anything which he had anticipated. Serious purpose takes the place of clownish antics, and the spirit of the buffoon is completely forgotten in the lofty thoughts of men who invoke the blessing of God upon the work in which they are engaged. And surely, if the entrance of the candidate, the benefit of the lodge prayer, the solemn vow of fidelity, and the call to his noblest manhood to prove himself worthy of the badge of a mason, impress the postulant, he must be doubly impressed by the singularly beautiful charge which is addressed to him as he stands in the N.E. Corner, in the shoes of all the millions who have gone before him, figuratively, as each one of them in turn had done, to represent the stone upon which the whole structure depends for its stability? By this time it must have been borne in upon him that the Society of which he has become a member cherishes noble aims, exists to inculcate lofty thoughts, and, as he knows that the strength of a chain is the strength of its weakest link, so he must recognize that Freemasonry expects every one of its members to represent a stone perfect in all its parts, and fitted to fill its place in the vast temple of universal brotherhood which every succeeding generation of Craftsmen strives to carry nearer to completion.

In popular parlance the exhortation delivered at the N.E. Corner is called "the Charity charge," and if one considers the older meaning – the New Testament meaning – of the word the term is singularly appropriate. For charity meant love towards our fellow men – the chief of the Christian graces – and love is the foundation on which every Mason must build if he would be faithful to the divine purpose of the Architect of our Mysteries. But, with the passing of the years, charity has lost its original meaning, and, in every day speech, has come to connote merely monetary or other material relief or assistance. Thus to restrict its significance is to deprive the word of some of its grandeur, and I often think that the author of the finely-phrased charge which is delivered in all our lodges today took a narrow view of the matter, and in a somewhat unworthy way limited a spacious subject. He confines it wholly to pecuniary assistance, emphasizing its highest note by contrasting rank and riches with the depths of poverty and distress; and this view is further impressed upon the mind of the initiate by the custom of thrusting a donation-box before him, and calling upon him to subscribe from an empty pocket. I think the practice is just a trifle theatrical, not altogether dignified, and, as the man's purse has been deliberately emptied before hand, practically useless as an illustration of the need for being ever ready to help a poor and distressed brother. The conventional charge does less than justice to the genius of Masonry, and, as though conscious of this, some brethren seek to relieve its single purpose, and widen its scope, by the introduction of a passage from another source.

"Benevolence," they say, "attended by heaven born Charity is an honor to a nation whence it springs, is nourished, and cherished. Happy is he who has sown the seeds of Benevolence in his breast; he envy not his neighbor, he believeth not a tale when told by a slanderer. Malice and revenge having no place in his breast, he forgives the injuries of men."

Elsewhere in our ceremonial there is evidence that the Charge is not wholly to refer to pecuniary assistance. In the final Exhortation of the Degree there is reference to the ceremonies which are so amply illustrated in the N.E. Corner, namely Benevolence and Charity, which clearly indicates, I think, that the matter is not to be circumscribed by mere money. Indeed, although we thus insist on expounding charity at all our meetings, it is our boast that we never dispense charity. In the common acceptation of the term, charity is something just a little, if, indeed, any better than pauper relief – the crumbs which fall from a rich man's table to the dogs, the dole thrown to the beggar, the largess given by people of means ostensibly for the benefit of the poor, but really, as a rule, because their doing so gives them admission to the goodwill of the public. That is not the Masonic way if I apprehend Freemasonry aright. The Mason helps out of kindness of a generous fraternal heart, never forgetting that the poor and distressed recipient is a brother with a well-founded claim to compassionate consideration. He does not parade his benevolence in the market place, but respecting a brother's feelings, gives with a secret hand, praying that the world may never learn of what after all, is not the world's business. All this indicates, I think, that charity, as it is generally understood, is alien to the spirit of Freemasonry, and that the Charity which is inculcated in the N.E. Corner is something wider, and deeper, and grander than casual dispensing of pecuniary help.

If we take the other meaning of the word – "love towards our fellow-men" – we see the whole plan of Masonry revealed in a moment, and where, I suggest, could the plan be more fittingly unfolded than at the spot where the foundation stone of all stately and superb edifices is laid? The Freemason is engaged in the erection of the most magnificent of all structures – The Temple of Character – and ere he is equipped with tools, and invited to take a share in the work, it is well that he should know on what foundation he is expected to build.

An old and now forgotten book on Freemasonry lays it

down that the principal steps of the ladder that reaches from earth to heaven are Faith, Hope, and Charity of which Charity possesses the highest and most distinguished rank, and the reason for this will be evident, says the author, if we distinctly consider the exclusive properties of these virtues, and thence deduce the incomparable excellence of universal charity. Pursuing his plan he argues that Faith is a firm and sincere assent to the fundamental truths of religion. Hope is an earnest and well-assured expectation of escaping threatened dangers, and obtaining promised rewards, while "Charity in its greatest latitude, is an ardent love of God, united with the unfeigned affection for all his creatures. The love of God naturally inspires the love of our brother, created by the same Architect, formed of the same clay, springing from the same common parent, and cemented by the most indissoluble ties. The love of our brother is one of the principal conditions of our initiation into God's friendship, who is the Father and generous preserver of us all. Hence, if the vivifying beams of God's love be not shed abroad in the heart, there will exist little fraternal affection; but the common bond of Masonry and religion being violated, there can be no hopes of good fruit proceeding from so impure a stock, and thus both are calumniated from the vicious conduct of some of their professors. Charity is not capable of a more restricted sense; for, if it be disunited from the love of God, and understood simply of brotherly love, it would be a virtue of inferior rank, and must yield precedence to both faith and hope. But consider Charity in its most extended signification as the pure and unfeigned love of God and man, and the doctrine of Masonry, corroborated by the argument of St. Paul, will be fully understood and admitted."

Faith, he concludes, is the base; Hope is the column, and Charity the ornamental capital which comprises the fabric.

Long ago, Thomas a Kempis, in one of his many moments of inspiration wrote, "He is truly great who hath a great charity," and it was probably with some thought such as that in his mind that Carlyle said, "Infinite is the help that man can yield to man." A great charity, and a great field in which to exercise it! The one is what the Freemason is taught by every symbol of his faith to cherish; the other is the avenue by which he may prove his right to be called a brother.

I have said that "love towards our fellow-men" reveals the whole plan of Masonry, and that is why I think charity may be regarded as the brightest gem in the Mason's crown. It has been said that love is the food of the soul; Burton describes it as "that Homer's golden chain which reacheth down from heaven to earth, by which every creature is annexed, and depends upon his Creator," and if Burton had been a Mason he would probably have ornamented his metaphor with symbols of the Craft. Given the will to achieve its end, Freemasonry could become the greatest power in the world for good, banish strife, and envy, and malice, and a hundred other things that hinder humanity in its progress towards perfection.

May not we take from all this that every Lodge should be a shrine at which the faithful Mason may burn tapers to friendship, kindliness, goodwill, and all the other virtues that are comprehended in the phrase "love towards our fellow-men?" Within the sanctuary of the Lodge a brother may find that peace which is denied to him in the outer world. This is finely expressed in a charge of one of the higher degrees. After exhorting the brother to faithful service, the Charge proceeds: –

"While such is your conduct, should misfortune assail you, should friends forsake you, should envy traduce your good name, and malice persecute you, yet may you have confidence that among Masons you will find who will administer relief in your distresses, and comfort in your afflictions."

You remember what Burns says in one of his early poems? –

The heart benevolent and kind
The most resembles God –

and Masons who work under the All-Seeing Eye of the Great Architect of the Universe, ever striving by thought, and word, and deed, to approximate nearer and nearer to Divine goodness, must recognize the truth of the poet's words.

And in the end charity is the only thing that counts. Love is the only coin that will be current at the last final reckoning when we shall be called to give an account of our stewardship. Wealth, position, earthly power – all will be as dust in the balance, and as the drop in the bucket. One of the grimmest legends I know is that of Charlemagne who made himself master practically of the whole world of his day. When he died he was buried at Aix-la-Chapelle. His dead body, arrayed in all the robes of Kingly grandeur, was seated on the Imperial throne. On his knees was placed the Volume of the Sacred Law, and there he sat in all the awful majesty of death with his dead finger pointing to the line in the Gospel according to St. mark, "What shall it profit a man if he gain the whole world and lose his own soul?" Brethren, it is possible for the faithful Mason to achieve that what Kings of the earth have failed to accomplish. Each of us may be a little center radiating the kindly influence of a sincere heart upon those around us, working often, if not, indeed, always, silently with never a thought of recognition, and finding that we are striving to be faithful to the principles of our Craft. One of the outstanding monuments of out history is the Temple at Jerusalem. You recall how it rose on Mount Moriah in silence without the sound of metal tool. Are not these silent builders of the house of God symbolical of all the good work of the world? The builders of character are forever at work. They slumber not nor sleep. But ever their work is done silently. And as the timbers came from Lebanon, the stones from the quarries, and the vessels from Zeredatha so from a thousand sources come the materials out of which character is built. The good we do to others, the influence we exert upon those around us, the friendships we inspire, the wisdom we glean from experience – all these are gathered by the unseen hand to form the intangible but eternal structure that shall bear witness as to what manner of men we are.

The great principle of love towards our fellow men, which is inculcated at the N.E. Corner, is emphasized in no unmistakable fashion in the Ancient Charges of Free and Accepted Masons which are appended to the Laws and

Constitutions of the Grand Lodge of Scotland. These charges, like Masonry itself, date from time immemorial and treat of the fundamental principles of the Order.

"Masons," say the Charges, "Unite with the virtuous of every persuasion in the firm and pleasing bond of fraternal love; they are taught to view the errors of mankind with compassion, and to strive, by the purity of their own conduct, to demonstrate the superior excellence of the faith they may profess. Thus Masonry is the center of union between good men and true, and the happy means of conciliating friendship amongst those who must otherwise have remained at a perpetual distance."

All through the Charges this insistence of brotherly love persists. "Masonry has ever flourished in times of peace and been injured by war, bloodshed and confusion;" says the author, "so that kings and princes, in every age, have been much disposed to encourage the craftsmen on account of their peaceableness and loyalty." Even when Masons have a difference, and when all means of friendly conciliation have failed, and they have to proceed to law to settle it, they are enjoined to "carry on their process, or law-suit, without wrath and rancor (not in the common way), saying or doing nothing which may hinder brotherly love and good offices to be renewed and continued, that all may see the benign influence of Masonry, as all true Masons have done from the beginning of the World, and will do to the end of time."

I cannot but think that if in thought we take our stand at the N.E. Corner from time to time and mediate upon the charge which is there delivered always, of course, with the wider meaning of charity in our mind which I have sought to express, we shall get a grander conception of what Freemasonry is, and be inspired to carry out its great principles in all our dealings with mankind. And we should never forget that our duty is not only to those who are members of our brotherhood. He is a poor Craftsman who is kindly only to those who are conversant with the use and meaning of the Compasses and Square. Our pilgrimage is always towards light, and it we gather something of the light that is revealed to us we must reflect it upon all who come in contact with us. Thus will the world know that Masonry is a heaven-born institution. There is a beautiful old legend of a hermit who forsook the garish show of the world to mediate upon God in the quietude of a cave on the East Coast of Scotland. In the immediate vicinity were jagged rocks that were dangerous to mariners, and many a frail bark went to destruction upon them. The good man was troubled by these disasters and at length hit upon the idea of a guiding light. Whenever, therefore, a storm broke upon the darkness, the hermit took his lantern and, pacing the rockbound coast, waved it as he went as a warning to any sailor at sea. Down through the centuries the memory of his kindly deed has survived a beautiful testimony to a heart large with love of his fellow men. The hermit may well be a symbol to the Freemason. Life is often likened to a sea in which the shoals and quicksand's and currents are poverty, distress, disease and affliction. If, in times of peril to others, the Craftsman sheds the kindly light of a generous heart he will, in very truth, build upon the foundation stone which is Charity, prove himself worthy of the name he bears, and, as Goldsmith has so beautifully said, *"learn the luxury of doing good."*

And it is with some thought such as that, that I would leave the subject.

> *In Faith and Hope the world will disagree, but all mankind's concern is Charity.*

wrote Pope; and in a very special sense it is the concern of the Freemason. And let us be charitable in all things, slow to think evil, quick to be jealous of the good name of a brother, ready to render every kind office of mercy that occasion may require. Let us look with a kingly eye upon a brother's shortcomings, and let us be ever charitable in judgment, and lenient in condemnation. It has been well said that there is nothing that is meritorious but virtue and friendship and, indeed, friendship itself is only part of virtue. Like rivers, and the strand of seas, and the air, friendship is common to all the world. Life should be fortified by many friendships; and where, one may reasonably ask, is the spirit more likely to be fostered than in the halls of Masonry? The wise king of Israel tells us in "Proverbs," that *"a friend loveth at all times, and is a brother born adversity;"* you remember that Shakespeare says –

The friends thou hast and their adoption tried,

Grapple them to thy soul with hoops of steel.

Pure friendship is something which men of an inferior intellect can never taste. It is a holy thing, not to be given lightly, and must rest on mutual goodwill and perfect trust. If we seek to instill something of this spirit into the apprentice as he stands at the N.E. Corner, we cannot fail to impress him with the majesty and inspiring grandeur of that which we call Freemasonry.

Religious and Masonic Symbolism of Stones

By William Wynn Westcott

As operative Masons are mostly concerned with preparing and shaping stones and with fixing them into buildings, so we Free and Accepted Masons are much concerned with the symbolic meanings which stones have received in the religious worship of all ages and peoples, and also in the emblematic uses of stones as exhibited in our ceremonies and rituals.

It has been found from the earliest times that men were disposed to erect stones to represent their gods, and from simple, unhewn stones we find they progressed to the use of hewn pillars, and still later to pillars fashioned by sculpture into the likeness of animals and men to become objects of reverence and worship as representing gods or deified ancestors. In later times, when the art of building had made progress, particular stones and portions of a building received special workmanship as well as particular names; for example, note the Corner Stone, the Key Stone, and the Cape Stone; and at last complete buildings of stone were erected for the worship of God - altars, temples and churches.

At the period of our Masonic Initiation we are made to represent the Foundation Stone always placed at the Northeast corner of the building; one side facing to the North representing darkness and ignorance, and. the other to the Rising Sun of knowledge in the East. This corner stone was and still is often laid with ceremonial forms, and beneath it were placed in olden times and also in our own days certain coins, metals and writings as a record of the foundation. Tacitus in his *Histories*, tells us that this function was duly performed at the rebuilding of the Capitol at Rome.

This Corner Stone is generally of cubical shape, and the symbolical explanation is that the square side represents Morality and the six sides of the cube refer to Truth looking in all directions.

In the Masonic Consecration of a Corner Stone it is customary to anoint with Corn to represent food necessary for work, with Wine for refreshment, and Oil for the well-earned rest after labor.

In our English Craft Masonry we note the three notable Pillars representing Wisdom, Strength and Beauty and the Ionic, Doric and Corinthian styles of architecture.

In Mark Masonry we are taught regarding the value of the Keystone. In medieval times workmen put each his own mark on squared stones, and it is suggested that keystones bore the marks of Overseers.

In the Royal Arch we hear not only of an arch and a keystone, but also of an Altar of white stone in the form of a double cube and upon it was engraved the Sacred Name.

The Most Excellent Masters' Lodge has reference to a Cape-stone. A. E. Waite notices a Scotch grade of Marked-Master whose legend narrates the fall of the Cape-stone or Coping-stone of the North Gate of the Temple of Solomon, which killed the Intendant of the works.

The Double Cube is a form of special excellence, and its side, often absurdly called the 'Oblong-square', is considered to be the proper form for a Masonic Lodge.

English Masons refer to the Rough Ashlar and the Perfect Ashlar; these are the unhewn block and the finished cube.

In earlier times some Lodges appear to have exhibited a peculiar stone, the Broached Thurne1, a name which has lately led to much controversy as to its shape, and the manner in which its surface has been worked: some authors have declared it to be the same as the Rough Ashlar because an old erroneous Ritual says it was for the Apprentice to work upon; while Mackey argued that it was a Perfect Ashlar; others again say it was a pyramid upon a cube. *Broach* is an old English word for *spire*, and is also the name of a tool for boring holes; *broached* also means a certain surface marking; *thurnel* is alleged to be a derivative from the Norman-French *tournelle*, a little tower or pyramid.

In Masonic symbolism the Rough Ashlar is said to represent Man in a state of nature, and the Perfect Ashlar, Man educated and intellectual.

There were in times past some critics who objected to the R. Arch legendary ritual on the ground that curved arches and the use of a Key-stone were unknown in Solomonic times - he is believed to have built his Temple in 1012 B.C.; but recent discoveries among the ruins of Egyptian tombs and temples have shown arches which are referred to 1600 B.C. as the date of their erection; the Key-stone is also found in arches among the ancient ruins of Peru and Mexico.

Referring again to rough and hewn stones it is curious to note that in Exodus xx, 25, we read that an altar must not be built of hewn stones; and again, Joshua raises an altar of 'Stones upon which no man has laid a tool' (Joshua viii, 31) the reason given being that men should not be encouraged to shape stones for religious purposes, lest they come to make statues of gods, and so become led into the worship of idols, which, however, all the races of the Holy Land were very prone to practice.

The Cubical stone receives a highly spiritualized symbolism in the Christian degrees of our order, notably in the Rose-Croix ritual which, referring in one point to failure, loss and despair, states that the Cubical stone pours forth blood and water; here it is taken reverentially as a symbol of the Crucifixion.

In theological works Christ is also referred to as the Corner Stone of the Church, the Cape Stone of the Church fabric and the Key (stone) of Heaven. The Old Testament had also, before the time of Jesus, used the term corner Stones to mean persons of eminence, and prophetically for the Messiah; in Isaiah xxvi, 16, we read of 'a Precious Corner Stone to be laid in Zion'.

The worship of stones as representing gods was perhaps the earliest form of religious observance; the stone from its solidity and durability would suggest the power and stability of a deity; stone worship has been traced in almost all lands and among almost all uncivilized races, and is hardly extinct even in our days. Certainly traces have been found in Europe within the last two centuries: Scheffer in 1673 describes the worship of an unhewn stone by Laplanders: Martin also found reverence given to a stone in the Western Isles of Scotland, the natives called it the Bowing-Stone; Roden relates that on the coast of Mayo in Ireland a sacred stone was carefully wrapped up in flannel, was brought out and adored at intervals, and was supplicated even in the last century by wreckers who prayed for a shipwreck upon their coasts. Borlase in his *History of Cornwall* also tells us that many persons there revered certain stones, approaching them at night with torches and prayers for material success.

In the Old Testament of the Hebrews we read that the patriarch Jacob set up a pillar of stone and anointed it with drink and oil as a religious action at Bethel, to commemorate the appearance of Jehovah to him in a dream, when he saw the ladder reaching from earth to heaven and received a special blessing (Genesis, xxviii). Jacob also set up a pillar as a witness of the covenant between Laban and himself (Genesis xxxi, 45); in chapter xxxv, 14, we read that Jacob set up another pillar in memory of a second appearance of Jehovah to him; and in verse 20 we read that Jacob set up still another pillar in memory of the death of his wife Rachel; this latter is perhaps the earliest mention of a Tombstone; and this example led to the reverence paid in later times to tombstones in relation to Ancestor Worship. So Jacob appears to have set up altogether four notable pillars. Joshua erected a monument of twelve stones at Gilgal; thus bane suggests a ring or circle.

Reference must be made to the two Tables of Stone, Exodus xxii and xxiv, on which were written the Ten Commandments of Jehovah; the first pair was broken by Moses; the second set was preserved in the Ark in Horeb, and was later on placed in the Temple of Solomon.

Note that the two pillars at the entrance of the Temple of Solomon were not of stone but of brass; they are said symbolically to represent the stone Pillars of Seth, Enoch and Hermes, of which many works make mention, but in regard to which I am unable to find any real information, although Josephus is said to mention them in his First Book of Antiquities, and two pillars erected before the Noachian Deluge are referred to in Ancient Masonic Charges, for example in the 'Cooke MS' of the 15th Century, it is narrated that all science was written upon each of two pillars, one of which could not be destroyed by fire, and the other not injured by water; the legend relates that after the Flood these two pillars were recovered by Hermes and Pythagoras and the inscriptions upon them formed the basis of all other knowledge.

Samuel erected a stone pillar between Mizpah and Shen and called it Ebenezer (the stone of help), I Samuel, vii, 12.

King Saul is said to have set up a pillar or monument at Carmel as a memorial of his success over the Amalekites. There was also the Pillar of Absalom which he raised to commemorate himself because his sons had died, 'and it is called Absalom's monument unto this day', II Samuel, xviii, 18. The Jewish historian Josephus said it was standing 'in the King's dale' in his time. Absalom was buried in a pit and a heap of stones was raised over his grave; this is perhaps the earliest mention of a funeral Cairn.

There are well known references to symbolic stones both in the Old and New Testaments. In the 118th Psalm we read: 'The stone which the builders rejected has become the head of the corner.' This is considered as prophetic of Jesus as the Christ who was rejected by the Jews but became the Head Stone of the Church. Jesus quoted these words in Matthew, xxii, and adds: 'He that falleth on this stone shall be broken to pieces, but on whomsoever it shall fall it will scatter him as dust.'

St Peter calls Jesus, in his first Epistle ii, 4, a precious stone and a living stone; while Peter was called *Cephas* - a stone - by Jesus himself, Matthew xvi, 18, and John i, 42.

In Revelation ii, 17, we read: ' To him that overcometh I will give him a White Stone and upon the stone a new name written which no man knoweth but he that receiveth it.' This is taken by the Church to mean a full pardon and absolution, and a reward of merit.

The prophet Zechariah had a vision of Joshua the High Priest with Satan standing beside him as an adversary; in *cap*. iv, we read of a very mysterious Stone: 'For behold the stone that I have set before Joshua, upon one stone are seven eyes.' The commentators declare this to refer to Christ the Messiah, to show by the number Seven His perfect wisdom.

True believers in Christ are called stones by the apostle Peter: 'Ye also as lively stones are built up a spiritual house.'

We may read in Job, chap. xxxviii, that the Almighty, speaking to Job, said: 'Where wert thou when I laid the foundations of the earth? Whereupon are the foundations thereof fastened? Who laid the corner stone thereof?'

The Old Hebrew writings of the Talmud and similar Rabbinical books have many references to this Stone of Foundation, called *Aben Shatijah*, which appears to have been at first only a symbol of the world's stability and not any actual stone or building; but as the years passed on the name became associated with legends of a real stone and was connected with the histories of Seth, Enoch, Jacob, David, Solomon and his First Temple, and then with Zerubbabel and the Second

Temple at Jerusalem. The medieval Rabbis declared that this sacred stone was transported to Spain, was thence carried to Ireland, placed in the Cathedral of Cashel, and upon it the Kings of Munster were crowned; it was there called Lia Fail, or Fatal Stone, and then on to Scotland in 513, where it was used as a Coronation Stone for Fergus, a Royal Prince, and for later Kings of Scotland, crowned at Scone. Our English King, Edward the First brought it to London in 1297, and this is the stone now preserved in Westminster Abbey upon which our kings and queens are crowned; its size is small and said to be 22 by 13 by 11 inches. Some persons believe this Coronation Stone to be the very Pillar of Jacob, and the sacred stone of the Temple at Jerusalem; but unbelievers declare that the Westminster Coronation Stone is of the sandstone formation of the West coast of Scotland and was quarried there. It is to be seen under the Coronation Chair in the Chapel of Edward the Confessor. England has also another Coronation Stone at Kingston-on-Thames; upon this stone several of the Saxon Kings were crowned. The Irish believe that they have still a royal stone embedded on the summit of the Hill of Tara in County Meath, and this is sometimes called Lia Fail or the Stone of Destiny. Tara was the capital and palace of the early Kings of Ireland, and a notable seat of learning.

Old Jewish legends narrate marvelous stores of the 'Stone of Foundation'; these are to be found in the *Toledoth Jeshu*, and in the Talmudic book *Yoma*. Prideaux's *Connection between the Old and New Testament* also refers to this stone, and some Masonic authors associate it with the double cube of our Royal

Arch Chapter legend, and declare that it had the Sacred Name of God engraved upon it, as the G.A.O.T.U.

Some of the Hebrew Rabbis of olden time who taught the doctrine of Metempsychosis, believed that a man's soul might after death not only be born again in a human body, but for its sins in an animal body, and even imprisoned in a *stone*. In the Hebrew *Emeh Hamelech* folio 153 we may read, 'the soul of a slanderer may be sent to inhabit a silent stone'. In the Old Testament Book of Habakkuk, ii, II, it is written, 'the stone shall cry out of the wall'. Rabbi Isaac Livria was once walking past the school house of Rabbi Jochanan at Tiberias and pointing to a stone in the wall said, 'In that stone is imprisoned a man's soul and it cries out for me to pray in its behalf.'

The Hebrew *Pesachim* says that God taught Adam to procure fire by striking *stones* together. The Rabbis had another quaint conceit about stones: we read in Genesis, xxviii, II, 'and he [Jacob] took from the stones [MABNI] of the place', and in verse 18, 'and 'he took the [ABN] stone'; they added, so the stones all rolled together into one stone for the saint to rest his head upon (Chullin, 91, 2.) *Note*: the English Bible gives 'one of the stones' in *v*. II - instead of the Hebrew words 'took of the stones'. In Leviticus, xxiv, we read that certain criminals were to be *stoned* to death, beyond the camp, notably any man who had cursed God.

The Chaldeans worshipped a mysterious stone called Mnizouris (see my edition of the *Oracles of Zoroaster*) and offered sacrifices to it.

The Phoenicians worshipped sacred stone pillars which were called Baetylia.

The Thebans of Greece worshipped Bacchus as a stone pillar, and Tacitus in his *History*, Book 2,3, tells us that at Paphos the goddess Venus was represented by a conical stone.

The Greeks used also to place Pillars, consecrated stones, before their temples and gymnasia, and even before the dwellings of the notables: Pausanias says that unhewn stones were preferred. Cybele, the goddess, was represented by a black stone; and Eusebius remarks that a black stone was peculiarly appropriate to a god because of his obscure and inscrutable nature. In a temple at Delos, Apollo is said to have been represented by a stone. Ovid tells us of Sisyphus, whose punishment was to roll a stone continually up a hill.

In the Roman Forum, among the remains of ancient times, there is the *Lapis niger* or Black Stone, said to mark the burial place of Romulus the First King of Rome.

The Roman god, Terminus, was represented as a stone, and so the pillar became used as a landmark.

Toland tells us the Druids showed great reverence for stones, and especially for upright pillars and for trilithons, such as are still to be seen at Stonehenge in Wiltshire, which has been considered as a center of the Solar Worship of the Celtic Druid priesthood. Much additional information may be found in *Irish Druids*, by James Bonwick, 1894.

Stone circles, dolmens, rocking stones and cromlechs once deemed sacred still exist, and there were also great stones with holes in them through which children were passed to ensure good fortune.

Bishop Schoning of Trondhjem states that in the 18th Century the people reverenced certain white stones, loaf-shaped, and bathed them with milk, anointed them with butter, and at Christmas times washed them with beer.

The Scandinavian *Edda* or book of legends refers to a Sacred White Stone which was venerated, and oaths were taken upon it.

Far in the wilds of Africa were found in the ruins of Zimbabwe curious stone pillars with bird-headed tops; these may have been related to Horus of Egypt, often seen hawk-headed.

The Roman Catholic Church found it difficult to abolish the worship of stones in Europe, and so several Church Councils condemned the practice; the Council of Arles held in 452, the Council of Tours in 567, Nantes, 658, and that of Toledo in 681. The Council of Tours ordered the exclusion from the Churches of all who venerated stones. We read also that Charlemagne, in the Eighth Century, and Canute in England, in the Eleventh, execrated the reverence for stones.

The most notable stone of the world is the Black Stone, preserved in the 'Kaaba' or Cubical House in the Court of the Sacred Mosque at Mecca, which is the Holy City of the Mohammedans. It is considered to be an aerolite or meteoric stone, and is now of a reddish black color; there is a legend that it was originally white. The Kaaba is a low tower about 40 feet high, with a flat roof, and it is covered by the Sacred Carpet made in Egypt once a year, and sent to Mecca to replace the one of the former year. Burckhardt in his *Travels in Arabia*, in 1815, says the Sacred Black Stone is only about seven inches in length, and of oval shape; it was broken during the siege of Mecca in A.D. 683, and was put together with cement and enclosed in a silver band. It is built into the wall at the northeast corner of the Kaaba, at a height suitable for men to kiss it in adoration. This stone or a similar one called Al-Lat was deemed a holy relic by the Arab tribes even before the time of Mahomet, and was associated with the history of Abraham and the casting out of Hagar and Ishmael, the bond-woman and her son, when preference was given to the free woman Sarah and her son Isaac. As already stated, Jerusalem had in its temple also a consecrated stone, and there is still a sacred stone in the Church of the Holy Sepulchure in that city which was once said to be the center or navel *Omphalos* of the earth, the Temple the navel of Jerusalem, and this stone the navel of the Temple.

The Temple at Ephesus was said to have had a sacred stone which had fallen from heaven - presumably a meteoric aerolite.

Among the Hindus we find the worship of white stone figures of the lingam and yoni, - an upright stone pillar standing in a cup, or on a flat dais. These are seen in fields, at the wayside and in temples from one end of India to the other; the worship of these is especially attributed to Saivas, that is, those who venerate Siva who is also called Mahadeva, he who destroys by changing. The Vishnuite reveres the Salagrama, a black pebble or a fossil ammonite (salagrama); they are nearly round and sometimes have perforations: the owner of one of these stones keeps it wrapped in a white cloth; he perfumes and bathes it occasionally and the water in which it has laid is drunk for its sin-removing properties. The Todas of Southern India worship stones and erect pillars and cairns wherever they dwell.

The Greeks and Romans of old had a custom of keeping stones, dies, or coins - tessara - as a token of friendship; and they also broke a tesseron or stone, and each of two friends kept a portion. The Hebrews, too, in early times, used a pledge called *Oirabon*, ORBUN, which was regarded as a sort of talisman to perpetuate friendship. The early Christians are said to have adopted this custom, and they marked their stones with the letters 'P.U.A.P.' meaning *Pater-* Father, *Uios-* Son, and *Agion pneuma-* Holy Spirit.

Mention must also be made of the 'Philosophers' Stone', the Stone of the Wise, in search of which so many students in past centuries have worked in vain, although there are many narratives in medieval tracts which declare the reality of such a stone and its discovery. There was a material aspect of the Stone by which it might transmute the baser metals into gold;

and there was a Spiritual Stone which should change the baser passions of men into aspirations towards the good and true. On the spiritual and metaphysical side Eliphas Levi and Hitchcock should be studied. On the material side countless methods for producing the Stone of Transmutation are recorded; the great problem was always, 'What is the Prima Materia to use?' and that procured, the processes should lead through stages of Blackness and Whiteness to the Red of Perfection; such a preparation thrown upon molten silver changed it into gold. In the Spiritual aspect the Red Stone is an emblem of Christ.

The Freemasons' system of the ballot seems to be a copy of the method of voting used in Ancient Greece, where small stones (*psephoi*), some black and some white in color, were used for voting purposes in their Law Courts, and at election to several offices. The White Stone then as now signified approval, and the Black rejection. At a later date the Romans also adopted this method of voting by stones.

In medieval mystical writings we find many references to the Smaragdine or Emerald Tablet of Hermes, a slab of green stone upon which were engraved the foundation tenets of alchemy; for which see the Latin work of Athanasius Kircher, *Oedipus Aegyptiacus*.

Reference may here be made also to certain stones used in divination by crystal-gazing; the British Museum has the 'Shew-Stone' of the famous Dr. Dee, who has left us a large volume of his relations with certain spirits. Lady Blessington, famous for beauty and culture in the last century, possessed a magic stone which had a great notoriety. The stone called beryl is said by some medieval authors to be the most suitable stone with which to see clairvoyantly.

Among the long-lost secrets of the ancients is the identity of a certain Stone found at Memphis in Egypt, described by Pliny, *Hist. Nat.* 38,7, and by Dioscorides, Book 5, who say that if it were ground to powder and applied to a part of the body; all sense of pain was removed, even that of surgical operations.

These notes upon stones, material and symbolic, might be extended indefinitely, but perhaps enough has been said as an introduction to a study of the symbolic meanings and uses of stones in Religion and freemasonry.